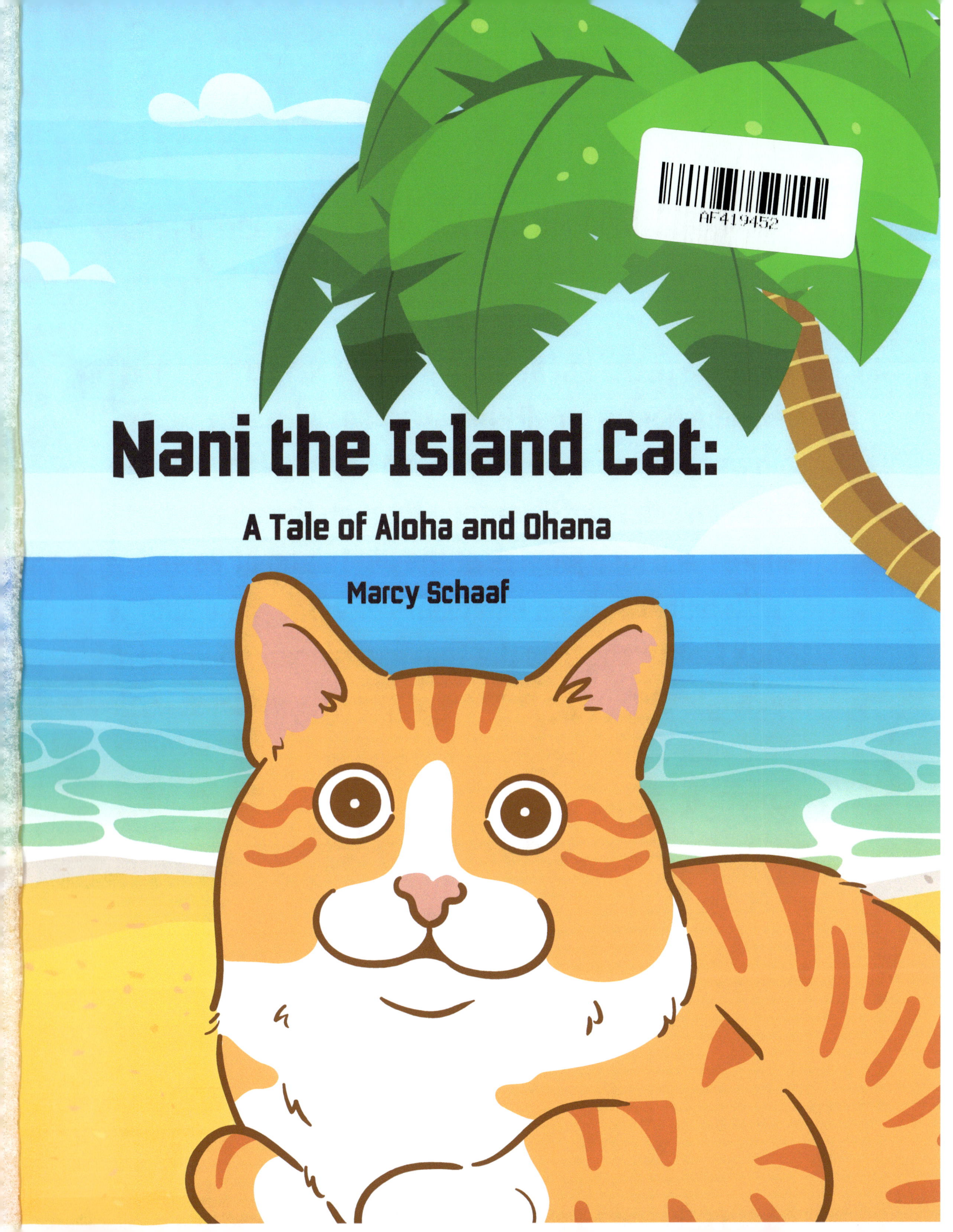

Nani the Island Cat:
A Tale of Aloha and Ohana
Marcy Schaaf

Title: Nani the Island Cat: A Tale of Aloha and Ohana

Introduction:
Welcome to the enchanting world of Nani the Island Cat! Join Nani, a small kine stray cat with a heart as big as the ocean, and her loving companion Auntie Leilani on a delightful journey through the sun-kissed shores and lush jungles of the Big Island of Hawaii. With laughter, love, and plenty of aloha, Nani and Auntie Leilani show us the true meaning of ohana and the magic of friendship. So grab a coconut drink, kick off your slippahs, and get ready for a purr-fectly charming adventure that will warm your heart and make you say, "Mahalo, Nani!"

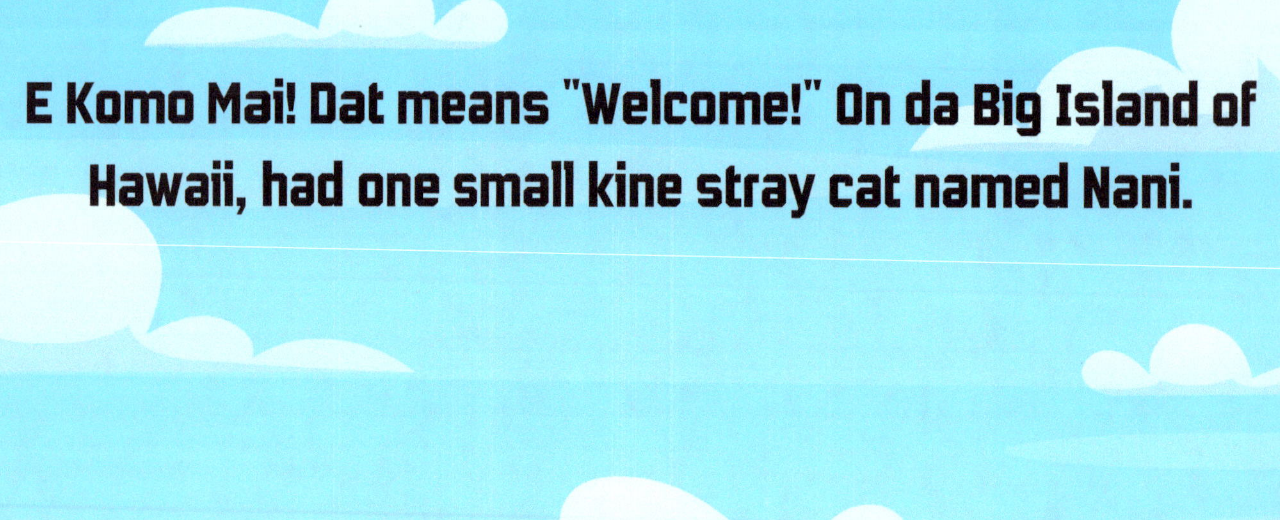

E Komo Mai! Dat means "Welcome!" On da Big Island of Hawaii, had one small kine stray cat named Nani.

Nani, she wen walk da streets, looking for ono grinds and one cozy spot fo' crash, but life on da streets was ha'a.

Every day, Nani had to watch out fo' fast cars and hungry predators, but she neva give up hope.

One sun-kissed day, Nani, she find one cozy hale nestled
between da palm trees, wit one kind wahine inside.

Da wahine, her name Auntie Leilani, she was a bit lonely before Nani showed up, but she welcomed her with open arms and one warm heart.

Nani, she finally get one hale kipa, and da adventure neva pau. Auntie Leilani and Nani had all kine fun tings fo' do!

Nani, she loved fo' play wit da string, chasing 'em all around da hale, makin' Auntie Leilani laugh.

Auntie Leilani, she giggle and clap, sayin', "You one playful kitty, Nani! Mahalo for da fun!"

"Meow-velous, Nani!" Auntie Leilani would cheer, as Nani give one happy purr in return.

Nani, she was also one crackah hunter! She kept da hale free from pesky critters in exchange fo' hale kupa kipa.

Auntie Leilani, she would brag to all her friends, "Nani, she da best mouser on da whole island!"

Sometimes, Nani would bring Auntie
Leilani a present, like one lizard or a big,
fat bug. Auntie Leilani, she would
pretend to be all scared, but secretly,
she was impressed.

"Thanks, Nani, but I tink I'll pass on da bug sushi tonight,"
Auntie Leilani would laugh.

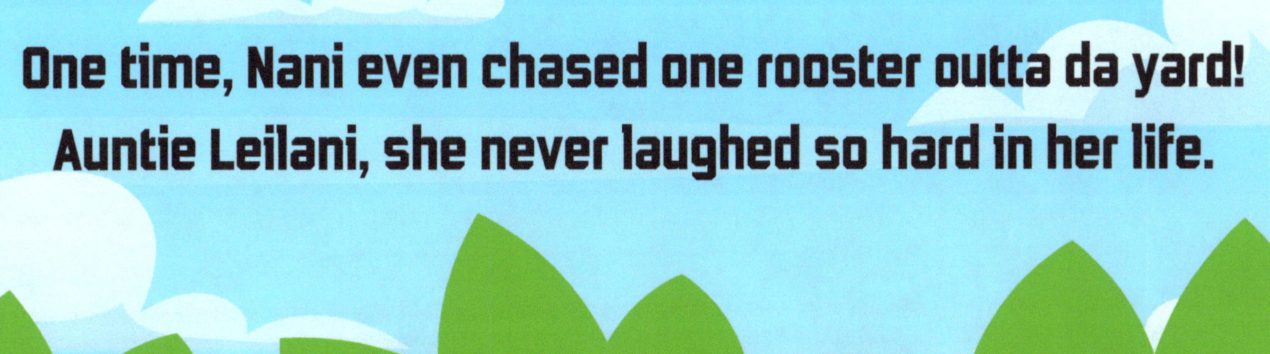

One time, Nani even chased one rooster outta da yard!
Auntie Leilani, she never laughed so hard in her life.

But not all da stray cats as lucky as Nani. Plenny still
wander da streets, trying fo' make it.

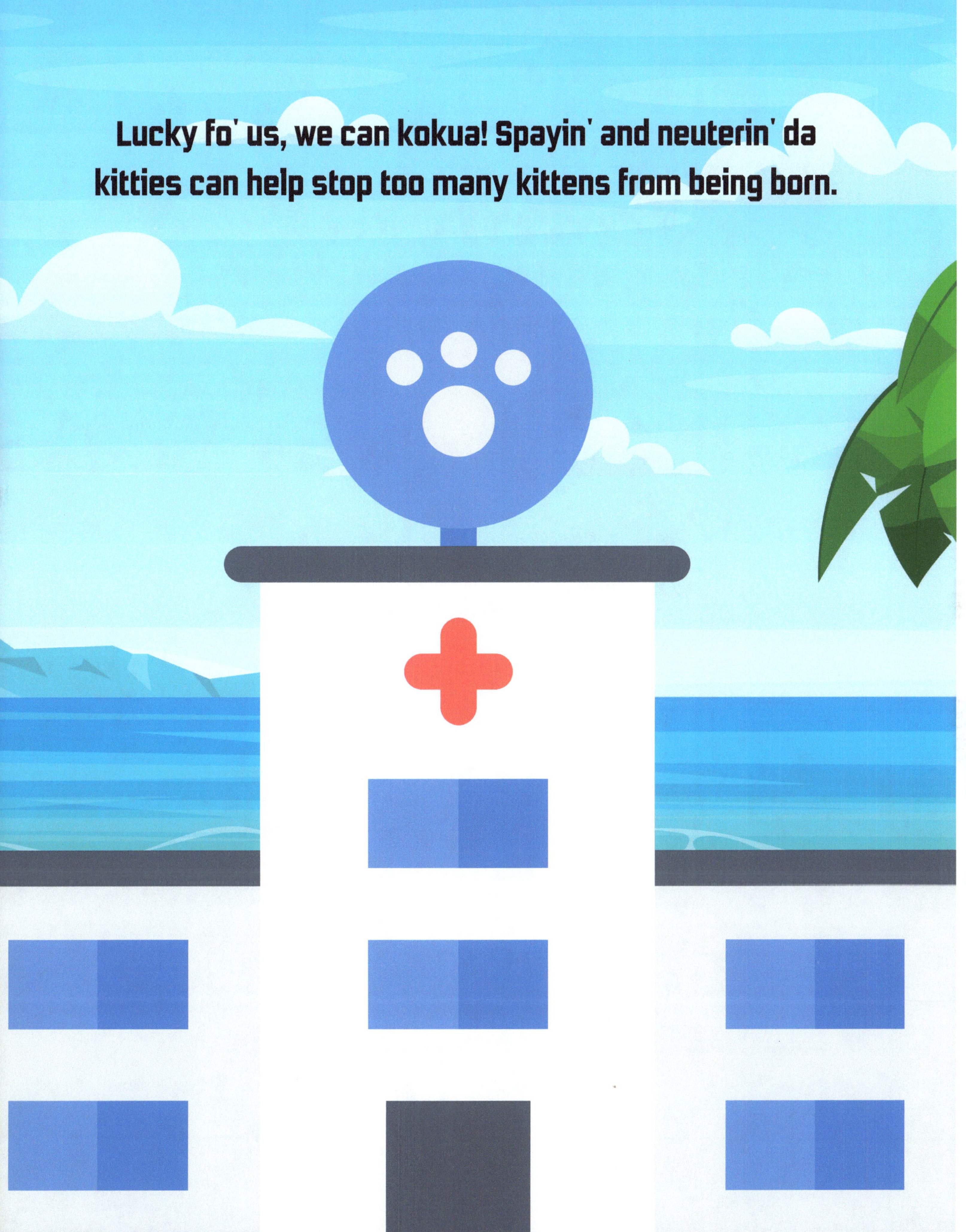

Lucky fo' us, we can kokua! Spayin' and neuterin' da kitties can help stop too many kittens from being born.

Feedin' da stray cats and givin' 'em shelter can make a big difference in their lives, yeah?

In return, these cats, like Nani, dey bring laughter and joy
to our homes and communities.

Dey not just cats; dey ohana, part of our island life.

Wit aloha and compassion, we can all make one big
difference in da lives of our furry ohana.

And as fo' Nani, she live happily eva afta, surrounded by love and endless bowls of fishy treats.

Auntie Leilani and Nani loved
makin' Spam Musubi together
and munchin' on 'em on da
porch swing.

Nani and Auntie Leilani would also spend lazy afternoons loungin' in da sun, listenin' to da sound of da waves crashin' on da shore.

Sometimes, they'd take long walks through da jungle, Nani ridin' on Auntie Leilani's shoulder, explorin' all da hidden treasures of da island.

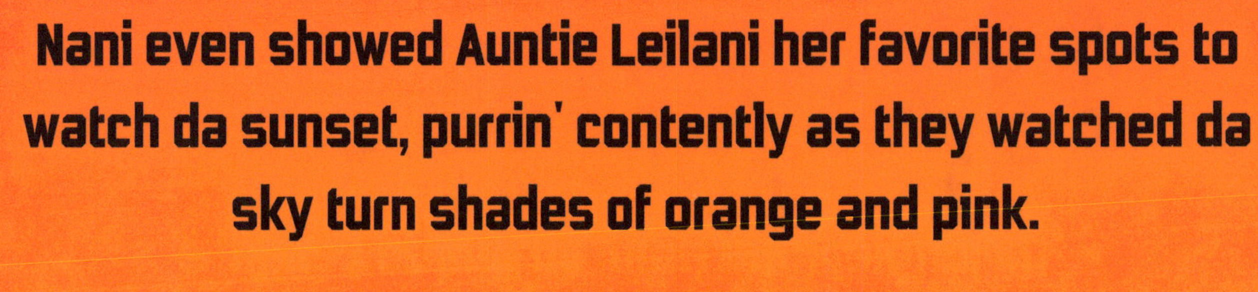

Nani even showed Auntie Leilani her favorite spots to watch da sunset, purrin' contently as they watched da sky turn shades of orange and pink.

When da moon was full, Nani would dance around da yard, chasin' shadows and makin' Auntie Leilani laugh with her silly antics.

And when it was time for bed, Nani would curl up next to Auntie Leilani, keepin' her warm with her soft fur and gentle purrs.

Together, Nani and Auntie Leilani made one purr-fect pair, bringin' joy and love to each other's lives every single day.

But their adventures didn't end there. They had many more stories to share, filled with laughter, love, and plenty of aloha.

And so, Nani and Auntie Leilani's bond grew stronger with each passing day, reminding us all of da power of ohana and da magic of friendship.

For on da Big Island of Hawaii, where da sun shines bright and da ocean sings its sweet melody, anything is possible when you have love in your heart and a furry friend by your side.

Da end.

The actual cat this story's about!

Author Bio: Marcy Schaaf

Marcy Schaaf is an avid storyteller and nature enthusiast who found inspiration in the vibrant landscapes and rich culture of the Hawaiian islands. In 2024, Marcy embarked on a journey to the Big Island of Hawaii, where she immersed herself in the island's beauty and embraced its spirit of aloha.

During her time on the island, Marcy fell in love with the warm hospitality of the locals and the mesmerizing sights of the tropical paradise. It was here that she encountered the heartwarming tale of Nani the Island Cat and Auntie Leilani, which inspired her to share their story with the world.

Drawing from her own experiences and the enchanting atmosphere of Hawaii, Marcy crafted a charming tale that captures the essence of aloha and celebrates the bond between humans and animals. Through her writing, Marcy hopes to spread joy and gratitude for the wonders of nature and the power of friendship.

When she's not writing, Marcy can be found exploring the great outdoors, capturing the beauty of the natural world through her photography, or curling up with a good book and her own furry companions. She currently resides in the Pacific Northwest, where she continues to find inspiration in the wonders of the natural world.

Spam Musubi

Spam musubi is a popular Hawaiian snack that has become a beloved household staple in many Hawaiian homes. This tasty treat consists of a slice of grilled Spam (a canned meat product) placed on top of a block of rice, all wrapped together with a strip of nori (seaweed). It's simple, yet incredibly flavorful and satisfying.

The origins of Spam musubi can be traced back to Hawaii's multicultural heritage. During World War II, Spam became a widely available and affordable food item in Hawaii, as it was a staple ration for American soldiers stationed in the Pacific. The local population, which included a diverse mix of ethnic groups, embraced Spam as a versatile ingredient that could be incorporated into various dishes.

Over time, Spam musubi emerged as a popular snack that reflects the fusion of Hawaiian and Asian culinary influences. It combines the convenience of American canned meat with the traditional Japanese technique of wrapping rice with nori. This combination of flavors and textures creates a delicious and portable snack that is perfect for enjoying on the go or as a quick bite at home.

In Hawaiian households, Spam musubi is often made in large batches and stored in the refrigerator for quick and convenient snacking. It's a favorite choice for school lunches, picnics, beach outings, and family gatherings. Additionally, many local eateries and convenience stores in Hawaii offer their own variations of Spam musubi, showcasing the snack's enduring popularity and cultural significance.

Overall, Spam musubi has become deeply ingrained in Hawaiian culinary culture, serving as a tasty reminder of Hawaii's diverse heritage and the resourcefulness of its people.

Books By Schaaf

www.BookBySchaaf.com

Find us at: